The Blunders *of our* Governments

ANTHONY KING

&

IVOR CREWE

ONEWORLD

A Oneworld Book

Published by Oneworld Publications 2013

Copyright © Anthony King and Ivor Crewe 2013

ISBN 978-1-78074-266-3
eISBN 978-1-78074-267-0

Typeset by Tetragon, London
Cover design by Stuart Polson
Cover illustrations by Matthew Buck at Hack Cartoons
www.mattbuckhackcartoons.com

Printed and bound by
CPI Group (UK) Ltd, Croydon, CR0 4YY

Oneworld Publications
10 Bloomsbury Street, London WC1B 3SR

To our colleagues over many years in the Department of Government at the University of Essex